21st Century
Basic Skills
Library

YOUR HEALTHY PLATE
PROTEIN

3

by Katie Marsico

Cherry Lake Publishing • Ann Arbor, Michigan

CHERRY LAKE Publishing

Published in the United States of America
by Cherry Lake Publishing
Ann Arbor, Michigan
www.cherrylakepublishing.com

Content Adviser: Theresa A. Wilson, MS, RD, LD, Baylor College of
Medicine, USDA/ARS Children's Nutrition Research Center, Houston, Texas

Photo Credits: Cover page 1, ©Celso Pupo/Shutterstock, Inc.; page 4,
©Photoeuphoria/Dreamstime.com; page 6, ©Robyn Mackenzie/
Shutterstock, Inc.; page 8, ©Marie C Fields/Shutterstock, Inc.; page 10,
U.S. Department of Agriculture; page 12, ©Joyfuldesigns/Dreamstime.
com; page 14, ©Zurijeta/Shutterstock, Inc.; page 16, ©Lisovskaya
Natalia/Shutterstock, Inc.; page 18, ©Larina Natalia/Shutterstock, Inc.;
page 20, ©Monkey Business Images/Shutterstock, Inc.

Library of Congress Cataloging-in-Publication Data
Marsico, Katie, 1980–
  Your healthy plate. Protein/by Katie Marsico.
    p. cm.—(21st century basic skills library. Level 3)
  Includes bibliographical references and index.
  ISBN 978-1-61080-349-6 (lib. bdg.)—ISBN 978-1-61080-356-4 (e-book)—
ISBN 978-1-61080-403-5 (pbk.)
  1. Proteins in human nutrition—Juvenile literature. I. Title. II. Title: Protein.
  TX553.P7M37 2012
  613.2'82—dc23   2011034821

Cherry Lake Publishing would like to acknowledge
the work of The Partnership for 21st Century Skills.
Please visit www.21stcenturyskills.org for more information.

Printed in the United States of America
Corporate Graphics Inc.
January 2012
CLSP10

TABLE OF CONTENTS

5   **What Is Protein?**

11   **Why Do You Need Protein?**

13   **Why Else Should You Eat Protein?**

17   **How Much Protein Do You Need?**

22   Find Out More

22   Glossary

23   Home and School Connection

24   Index

24   About the Author

What Is Protein?

Do you eat chicken? How about beans?

These foods have **protein**, which helps you grow healthy and strong!

Many foods, including meat and fish, have protein in them.

Poultry such as chicken and turkey also have protein.

Eggs are another excellent source of protein.

7

What other foods have protein in them?

Nuts and seeds do.

You can eat a handful of walnuts, sunflower seeds, or almonds. Beans have protein, too.

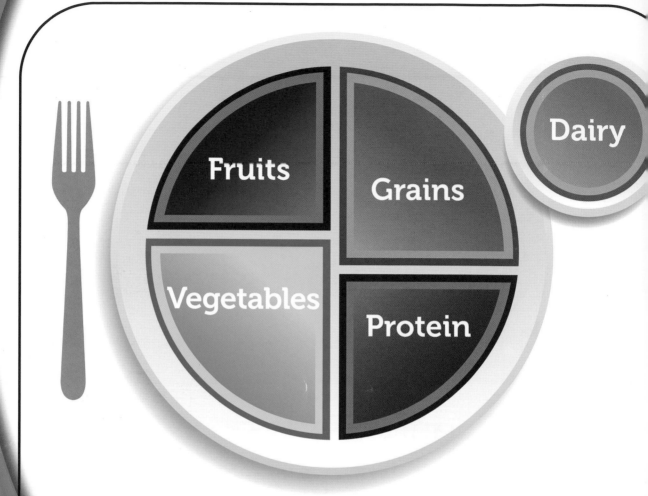

ChooseMyPlate.gov

Why Do You Need Protein?

Protein is one of five main **food groups**. All five groups are part of a **balanced diet**.

Protein is a **nutrient**. Nutrients give you **energy** and help your body grow.

Why Else Should You Eat Protein?

Protein makes up much of your body.

Most of the protein in your body is in your muscles. Your skin, hair, and fingernails are also made of protein!

Your body uses protein to do many different jobs.

Protein helps your body use energy. It also helps your body make blood and heal injuries such as cuts and scrapes.

How Much Protein Do You Need?

You should eat protein every day.

You can get a day's worth of protein by eating a small steak.

You can also eat a **serving** of beans or an egg.

Eating fish and poultry is a healthy way to add protein to your diet. If you eat red meat such as steak, make sure it is **lean**.

Peanut butter is also a tasty choice!

Talk to an adult about other healthy foods. Ask which foods have protein in them.

How will you put protein in your diet today?

Find Out More

BOOK

Schaefer, Lola. *Meat and Protein*. Chicago: Heinemann Library, 2008.

WEB SITE

United States Department of Agriculture (USDA)—Food Groups: Protein Foods

www.choosemyplate.gov/foodgroups/proteinfoods.html

Learn more about protein and how to make it part of your diet.

Glossary

balanced diet (BAL-uhntzt DYE-it) eating just the right amounts of different foods

energy (EN-ur-jee) strength needed to be active and alert

food groups (FOOD GROOPS) groups of different foods that people should have in their diets

lean (LEEN) having little or no fat

nutrient (NOO-tree-uhnt) a substance in food needed by people to stay strong and healthy

poultry (POHL-tree) farm birds such as chickens and turkeys that are raised for food

protein (PROH-teen) a nutrient that helps your body do many different jobs that keep it healthy and strong

serving (SURV-ing) a set amount of food

Home and School Connection

Use this list of words from the book to help your child become a better reader. Word games and writing activities can help beginning readers reinforce literacy skills.

a	choice	give	main	put	today
about	cuts	groups	make	red	too
add	day	grow	makes	scrapes	turkey
adult	diet	hair	many	seeds	up
all	different	handful	meat	serving	use
almonds	do	have	most	should	uses
also	eat	heal	much	skin	walnuts
an	eating	healthy	muscles	small	ways
and	egg	help	need	source	what
another	eggs	helps	nutrient	steak	which
are	else	how	nutrients	strong	why
as	energy	if	nuts	such	will
balanced	every	in	of	sunflower	worth
beans	excellent	including	one	sure	you
blood	fingernails	injuries	or	talk	your
body	fish	is	other	tasty	
butter	five	it	part	the	
by	food	jobs	peanut	them	
can	foods	lean	poultry	these	
chicken	get	made	protein	to	

Index

balance, 11
beans, 5, 9, 17
blood, 15

chicken, 5, 7

diet, 11, 19, 21

eggs, 7, 17
energy, 11, 15

fingernails, 13
fish, 7, 19
food groups, 11

hair, 13
healing, 15

lean meat, 19

meat, 7, 17, 19
muscles, 13

nutrients, 11
nuts, 9, 19

peanut butter, 19
peas, 9
poultry, 5, 7, 19

seeds, 9
servings, 17
skin, 13

turkey, 7

About the Author

Katie Marsico is an author of nonfiction books for children and young adults. She lives outside of Chicago, Illinois, with her husband and children.

24